Catherine Chambers | **How to get ahead in**

Retail

www.raintreepublishers.co.uk

Visit our website to find out more information about **Raintree** books.

To order:

☎ Phone 44 (0) 1865 888113

▤ Send a fax to 44 (0) 1865 314091

💻 Visit the Raintree bookshop at **www.raintreepublishers.co.uk**
to browse our catalogue and order online.

First published in Great Britain by Raintree,
Halley Court, Jordan Hill, Oxford OX2 8EJ,
part of Harcourt Education.
Raintree is a registered trademark of
Harcourt Education Ltd.

Editorial: Melanie Waldron, Lucy Beevor,
and Kate Buckingham
Design: David Poole and Calcium
Picture Research: Ruth Blair
and Maria Joannou
Production: Huseyin Sami

Originated by Chroma Graphics
Printed and bound in China
by South China Printing Company

10 digit ISBN 1 406 20446 3
13 digit ISBN 978 1 4062 0446 9

11 10 09 08 07
10 9 8 7 6 5 4 3 2 1

British Library Cataloguing in Publication Data
Chambers, Catherine
Retail. – (How to get ahead in)
381.1'02341
A full catalogue record for this book is
available from the British Library.

Acknowledgements
The publishers would like to thank the
following for permission to reproduce
photographs: Alamy Images pp. **17**
(Bob Johns/expresspictures.co.uk), **23**
(Cephas Picture Library), **25** (David Sanger
Photography), **37** (Image 100),
10 (Tina Manley), **44** (Adams Picture Library);
Amazon.co.uk p.**44**; Corbis pp.**33**
(Chuck Savage), **34** (David Pollack),
36 (George Disario), **4**, **26** (Reuters)
28 (Strauss/Curtis), **30** (Kim Kulish);
Empics p.**46** (Chris Ison/PAPhoto);
Getty Images pp. **21** (Photonica), **40**
(Stone/Alan Thornton), **42** (Stone/David
Roth), **14** (Stone/Ryan McVay), **9** (Taxi/David
Oliver), **51** (The Image Bank/Sean Justice),
39 (The Image Bank/Yellow Dog Productions);
Photolibrary p.**45** (Creatas); Rex Features
pp. **29** (Frank Monaco), **19** (John Downing),
8 (John Powell), **7** (Stuart Clarke).

Cover photograph of wooden coat hangers,
reproduced with permission of Alamy/
Andrew Paterson.

Author acknowledgements
Many thanks to the following for their
contributions to this book: Elaine Oliver of
New Look Retailers Ltd; Mary Forbes, Annette
Innes, Jane May and Jo Taylor of Ponden Mill
Ltd; and Mel Pye of Neet Feet. Thanks always
to John King - for his help, and so much more.

Contents

Introduction: The world of retail 4

Chapter 1: Is retail for you? 6

Chapter 2: Starting out 9

Chapter 3: Climbing the ladder 15

Chapter 4: Keeping things safe 20

Chapter 5: The product 23

Chapter 6: From warehouse to store 32

Chapter 7: Recruitment and training 37

Chapter 8: Going it alone 41

Chapter 9: Onwards and upwards 45

Further information 52

Glossary 54

Index 56

Words appearing in the text in bold, **like this**, are explained in the glossary.

The world of retail

Would you like to do a job that brings a smile to people's faces and where every day is different? Where your enthusiasm and energy really matter? Where a vast range of positions and opportunities are available to you? Where your social skills are valued as much as your school qualifications and where each day can make a difference to the success of your workplace? If the answer is "Yes!" to all of these, then a job in retail could be just right for you.

Where in the world?

The world of retail is enormous. Your skills will be snapped up wherever you go. You can work anywhere in the country. If you are good at a foreign language, then you could work abroad. The retail sector is one of the world's largest employers and is often one of the most successful in a country's economy.

below: *Retail workers all over the world try to make shopping a pleasure for their customers and profitable for their company.*

The USA has the largest economy in the world – and retail is its second-largest sector, taking nearly $4 trillion in sales every year. Almost 12 per cent of all US workers are employed in retail.

Some retail companies are huge. Wal-mart, a US company, is the leading retailer in the world, followed by the French company Carrefour. Wal-mart employs over a million people in the USA, and another 450,000 internationally. The second-largest retail company in the USA is Gap.

Who does what?

There is something for everyone who wants to work in retail. There are lots of opportunities for you to use a diverse range of skills. However, with everything you do – from the warehouse to the shop floor – it is always the customer who comes first.

Chain store and supermarket positions

Positions in retail depend on the size of the shop and whether or not it is part of a chain. The table below shows the various positions available in chain stores and supermakets.

below: *This table shows the wide variety of jobs available in the retail industry.*

Job location	Job titles
In-store	replenishers, sales advisers/assistants, administration and cash office personnel, shop-floor and department supervisors, assistant managers, managers, area managers, regional managers
Warehouse (distribution)	warehouse loaders and drivers, transport and **logistics** clerks, supervisors, distribution managers
Head office	buyers, **merchandisers**, visual merchandisers, area managers and regional managers, directors of retail operations, managing directors

Chapter 1

Is retail for you?

Let's turn this on its head. When you go shopping, what do you hope for as a customer?

Expectations

Do you have high expectations of:

◎ the staff serving you – their attitude and advice?

◎ what's on the shelf – the quantity, quality, and range?

◎ keen pricing and attractive offers?

◎ the ordering service?

◎ displays?

◎ **point-of-sale** and clarity of pricing?

◎ **aftercare** – the returns and complaints policy and procedure?

If you do, then ask yourself how well your expectations are met by the stores that you normally shop in. Which stores meet these expectations? Would you like to make these things happen to your own high standard? If so, one of the jobs in this book could be for you!

Qualifications

Retail qualifications are likely to help you through your retail career. They show that you actually know how to do the job, not just the theory behind it. A list of qualifications is shown below, and there are qualifications and courses mentioned throughout this book. You can get detailed information by looking at college websites.

NVQs/SVQs

National Vocational Qualifications (NVQs) and **Scottish Vocational Qualifications** (SVQs) are more practical and less academic than A- levels. They provide a flexible approach to studying a number of different subjects and allow you to progress at your own pace. Below are examples of the grades and what they represent in the area of retail operations.

◎ Level 2 is designed for shop-floor workers. The coursework involves everything from receiving goods and materials into storage to processing cheques and credit card transactions. There are compulsory (required) modules and several optional ones. Level 2 is equivalent to an A-level (England and Wales) or Higher (Scotland).

above: *Try to go to your local shopping centre at a quiet time and ask store supervisors about job opportunities.*

◎ Level 3 is designed for managers of small retail units or supervisors in department stores.
◎ Level 4 is designed for managers wanting to learn about **budgeting**, recruitment, and using resources effectively.

NVQ/SVQ Levels 2–4 arc also available in courses covering the following areas: Customer Service, Sales, Administration, Telephone Selling, Logistics, Distribution and Warehousing, and Call Handling.

Other qualifications

◎ **BTEC** First Diploma in Retail prepares you for NVQ Level 2. It includes Display Merchandising and Sales and Profit as core subjects. There are also specialized units in, for example, fashion retailing.
◎ BTEC National Award in Retail is equal to an A-level (England and Wales) or Higher (Scotland). It includes Marketing and **Promotion**, Retail Technology and Retail Finance.
◎ City and Guilds certificates are practical courses in everything from Security to Customer Service.
◎ **OCR** certificates in word processing skills and computer packages will help those wishing to enter the administrative side of retail, transport, and warehousing.

Get ahead!

Have a look at some adverts for job vacancies. See if you can find out how job opportunities differ in each of these retail areas:
• high street stores – including chain stores
• supermarkets
• **outlets**
• **concessions**
• owner/manager shops that are not part of a chain
• market stalls
• Internet shops
• call centres.

above: *Special annual promotions are slotted into the normal retail calendar.*

The retail calendar

If you want to work in retail, one of the most important things to understand is the retail calendar, which shows a peak in sales at Christmas. Companies often take 30 to 50 per cent of the year's profits at this time – or even more. Stores often have to take on extra staff in order to cope with the increase in trade. This could be good news for you, as Christmas staff are sometimes kept on when the store goes into the sale period in January. This means it is always worth doing your best, even if you are only on a short-term contract, as only the best staff are kept on.

Seasons in the store

During the January sales new spring stock starts to come in, especially for fashion and household goods such as furnishings, soft furnishings, wallpaper, and so on. Spring sales at Easter are often small, mid-term clear-outs, followed quickly by new summer stock. Summer sales start around July and in August, then back-to-school ranges start coming in at clothing shops and stationers. The new autumn/winter ranges follow, and then it is back full-circle to receiving Christmas stock around September/October. But whatever time of the year, every single day in retail is important. One good day can help balance out a bad day later on in the week.

It's all in the timing

Retail moves at a great pace, and each season is planned well in advance. If you want a summer holiday job, then apply in good time – probably from Easter onwards. Stores don't always advertise, so you might like to present your **curriculum vitae** (CV) and **covering letter** to store managers. There is more information about applying for jobs in chapter 9.

Chapter 2

Starting out

Where is a good place to start in retail? One of the best places is where most of the jobs are – on the shop floor, and in the stock rooms and offices behind the shop floor. There are many different retail environments, from small specialist shops to massive superstores. The secret of happiness and success is finding the right retail environment for you!

WHICH ENVIRONMENT?

Take a look at the different types and sizes of store in your nearest high street or shopping centre. Ask yourself what kind of environment you feel most comfortable in. Is it a large music store – part of a chain, with an exciting atmosphere and cutting-edge design? Or is it a small, quiet specialist shop – perhaps a florist's, a cricket gear store, or a chocolate shop!

Get ahead!

Try to get your 2-week work experience placement in a local store. Some schools also allow a **day-release** work experience scheme that takes place over a term. These are usually integrated with English, ICT, and personal development targets. Students are expected to present a report detailing their learning within the store. If you show real enthusiasm for retail, you could even be offered a Saturday job when you are 16.

below: *Try to get to know as much as you can about every product you stock. This will help you sell it.*

Replenisher

Replenishment is one of the most important jobs in retail. No shop can start the day without being well stocked. A large number of part-time, weekend, holiday, and Christmas jobs are in replenishment. It is one of the best ways of starting a career in retail. You will get excellent product knowledge and a real understanding of the importance of **product placement**, pricing, and offers.

Personal profile

◉ Methodical, accurate, with good organizational skills.

◉ Confident with basic arithmetic and paperwork. You might have to log off stock or check it on a computer.

◉ A sharp eye and cheerful nature. Things can get a bit hectic at times!

above: *If there is too much product for one part of the shelf, it has to be taken back to the stockroom and arranged in the same order as it is on the shop floor.*

What's in the job?

Replenishers don't only keep shelves well stocked. They also receive deliveries and check off stock against delivery sheets. In addition they return unwanted stock as "recalls" or "returns". This is all part of stock control, which is very important. Replenishers also have to price and sticker goods. They have to know when promotions begin, what they offer to the customer, and when they end. Replenishers often work outside trading hours, but can work during trading hours, too. In this case, they have to learn customer service skills.

Replenishment is a job in itself, but in smaller shops sales advisers often replenish. In many stores during the Christmas period and sales, everyone pitches in! Replenishers can be paid anything from the minimum wage to about £6.50 per hour. Night-time replenishers often get the best rates.

Routes to recruitment

Replenishment is often the first entry point into retail, and you can start at 16. Most employers want to see a good all-round education, with good **references**. ICT skills and evidence of basic maths skills are helpful. Any outside voluntary work such as helping to organize a club would add weight to your application.

THINKING AHEAD

You can work towards a supervisory role through experience and by obtaining NVQs in Retail Operations. This could also help towards getting a job in stock control and movement. Or, if you develop an interest in a particular type of stock, you might want to move onto the shop floor and try selling it.

Sales advisor

Are you keen to help people? Do you have a passion for a particular product? Can you multitask? If so, then why not try working as a sales advisor? It can be a really satisfying career choice for people who just like selling and working with the public. It is also a great start for those wanting to climb the retail career ladder. If you end up working in a company's head office, your experience as a sales advisor will help you understand exactly how tough it is on the shop floor at Christmas!

Sales advisor positions make good weekend and holiday jobs. As a temporary or part-time sales advisor you will grow in confidence and gain a wide range of skills. This will mean developing your experience of good customer service, selling skills, product and price knowledge, and keeping the stock tidy and attractive. You will also be on hand to find out about all the other types of jobs in retail. A good manager will see your enthusiasm and potential and help you move forward in the business.

left: *Some customers like to be shown different options. Others prefer to browse alone. A sales advisor has to learn to recognize what each customer wants.*

Personal profile

- You need to smile! smile! smile! It helps to create a buzz in the shop and will give you and your customers confidence. You also need good manners at all times. Many tricky situations can be solved quickly simply by remaining calm and polite.
- Good communication skills are essential. Sales advisors have to listen to what the customer needs, ask appropriate questions, and suggest options without being pushy.
- Teamwork, multi-tasking, and flexibility. These are very important in terms of hours and shifts worked, as well as duties carried out. You could be dusting shelves one minute and hauling them into the stock room the next. A few minutes later you might be brushing yourself down to do a shift on the customer service desk!
- You must be organized and methodical to be able to carry out all the different tasks on the shop floor, as well as meet excellent customer service standards.
- Engaging with the product, the company **brand**, promotions, and seasonal variations is very important. The more you find out about them, the better customer service you can give. And the more interesting your job will be.
- Understanding how the company operates is a big plus. Does it offer an ordering service, for instance? If so, you have even more choice to give your customer.

Get ahead!

Getting qualifications such as NVQs in Retail Operations and Customer Care will help you get started on the management ladder as a senior sales adviser. Level 3 qualifications can boost you forward into a supervisor's role. NVQs also help you to organize your work better and take a step-by-step approach to tasks and customer service. These kinds of skills and discipline help the shop to run smoothly and create a calm atmosphere. Customer Care qualifications can also help you move into call-centre selling, where your phone manner and **interpersonal skills** are hugely important.

What's in the job?

Most shop-floor jobs are divided into customer contact and tasks. But the amount of each depends on the size of the business, the way it is organized, and the nature of the product.

In a supermarket, you could be assigned till work, which always includes customer service. In a clothes shop, bookstore, chemists, or other chain or department store, you might help with replenishment and setting up promotions; work on the till and serve customers; order from and recall out-of-date products to the warehouse; collect, sort, and remove rubbish. Sales advisers are normally paid between the minimum wage and about £6.50 per hour to do these different tasks.

But you will have to remember that the customer is the focus of everything you do. Customer care is often randomly checked by "mystery shoppers". These are people employed by shopping centres and large companies to act as normal customers. They check that shops and their staff are reaching required standards and report their findings back to head office.

Routes to recruitment

A good basic education is helpful for a career in retail. GCSEs in Maths and English are generally required, although many sales assistants are employed without them. A GCSE in Business Studies can also be useful. Good knowledge of ICT will go a long way too! Tills are computers, and are increasingly high-tech. Of course good ICT knowledge is essential for working in computer retail.

left: *If things go wrong on a till it is important to remain calm and explain what's happening to the customer – with an apology and, of course, a smile!*

Chapter 3

Climbing the ladder

Are you already working part-time in retail? Even now, you can begin to climb the management ladder. Just ask yourself a few key questions. Are you keen to take a bigger part in decision-making? Are you pushing for that extra bit of responsibility? Do you want to help create a motivated team? Do you relish the thought of making your section, department or store look even better than it does already? If the answer is "Yes!" to all of these, then you are just the right material for a management position.

Supervisor

Your first step as a manager will probably be as a section or department head. You could then become a supervisor. Pay normally starts at around £5.50 per hour – although in some stores it can reach £7.00.

Personal profile
◎ A great teamworker.
◎ A good, calm delegator.
◎ An eye for detail – the store has to be presented professionally.
◎ Great organizational skills.
◎ Numeracy and literacy skills.
◎ Excellent interpersonal skills.

Routes to recruitment
Experience and a keen interest in the business will help you to become a supervisor. Make sure you work your way through the company grading scheme, if one exists. Doing a relevant NVQ to Level 3 will be helpful. There are also different grades of BTEC qualifications that can boost your chances in management.

It's up to you!

Make no mistake, a management position means that the buck really will stop with you! As a supervisor, you will answer to a store manager, but you will still share responsibility for customer satisfaction, store profit, accurate accounting, and powerful promotions. Keeping your staff happy and focused will also be up to you. This means that you must set clear goals for your staff on a day-to-day basis and on longer-term objectives. In addition you will help work out staffing levels and rotas to ensure a smooth-running shop.

CASE STUDY

Jenny Swales, Part-time supervisor

Jenny Swales began work in retail as a weekend worker at a large book and stationery chain in Bedfordshire. She was really keen to progress, and trained in-store to become a weekend supervisor. This included a training trip to the chain's head office. When Jenny left school, she began a degree in business and accounting. She managed to get a transfer to a large branch of the same chain store, and continued as a weekend supervisor. This helped her tight student budget! After university, Jenny decided that she enjoyed the financial side of retail more than the shop floor. She went into accounting, using both her degree and her retail experience.

Store manager

Do you want to manage a store and be responsible for absolutely everything – from store profit to staff rotas and store security? If something doesn't happen, then it is the manager's and no one else's responsibility to chase it up. On average an assistant manager's salary for a small store is between about £10,000 and £14,000 per year. This can reach up to £30,000 – or more in a department store. A manager can earn from £12,000 to £60,000 and above.

above: *Cash office procedures have to be followed perfectly in any business so that the company makes as much profit as possible.*

Personal profile

◎ Excellent organizational skills with the ability to think well ahead. This ensures a smooth rhythm to the running of the store. It gives your staff confidence, too.

◎ Ability to react quickly to changes. For example, you may receive a note from head office asking you to move whole areas of stock around to take advantage of a new promotion.

◎ Excellent people skills and the ability to delegate. These are essential skills to help you have a good performing store.

◎ Very good judgement of character. You will have to decide who to recruit in order to create a well-motivated, skilled team.

Jane May, Base Store Manager

Jane May is manager of a large store in Ashford, it is also the base store for a number of the chain's shops, spread over quite a wide area. This means that Jane has to help train managers within this area, track other stores' takings, and help to sort out their problems. As well as this, she keeps her own store to the highest possible standard.

How does Jane succeed? She says that in her job, you need to keep calm and work very, very hard! You need to know the strengths of your staff, and make sure they are happy, well motivated and up-beat. As base store manager, you also need a lot of company knowledge. Her biggest tip? Admit when you don't know something, and find out about it as soon as you can. Her greatest asset? Her assistant manager, Annette, who gives 100 per cent support, is on the same wavelength, but has huge strengths of her own.

What's next?

The sky is the limit for an experienced, successful, and dynamic store manager. Some go on to become area manager for a chain. This means they are responsible for a group of stores within a particular part of the country. An area manager's job will stretch all your multi-tasking skills, from chasing supplies to recruiting store managers. This could lead you right to the top of the tree as a retail sales director for the whole company.

If you work for an international retailer, you could become an overseas director. This means you would be responsible for setting up stores abroad. Inditex, with its well-known outlets such as Zara, is a good example of an international retailer. The company employs people from many parts of the world, and operates from Arteixo, Spain. So keep up those Spanish lessons!

above: *Managers should always be prepared to lead by example – get stuck in and do everything expected of the rest of the staff.*

Routes to recruitment

Many managers have worked their way to the top. Some have obtained qualifications – from NVQ Level 3 and BTEC National Awards to degrees. Some have none. Large chains and supermarkets now operate graduate training schemes for store managers. Retail, marketing, and business degrees are useful for getting on to these schemes. But other subjects are acceptable, too. There are now management entry schemes for people with A-levels (England and Wales), and Highers (Scotland).

CASE STUDY

Mary Forbes, Store Manager

Mary Forbes manages a busy, high-quality soft furnishing and bedding store in Dover. It is part of a large store chain. These are Mary's top tips:
- *Build a well-trained and customer-focused team of staff.*
- *Keep on top of product knowledge, special offers and good store presentation, so that customers are given the best service.*
- *Make sure that there is an on-going, high level of communication between head office and the store.*

Chapter 4

Keeping things safe

Are you very observant, with a good memory and a strong instinct about people? Are you fit, resilient, and a good team player? Then you might be interested in security work.

A well-organized security system is an important part of a good loss prevention policy. Loss prevention means protecting a company's profits and takes many forms including the reduction of theft. Profits help to expand a company, and can mean more job opportunities for everyone – including you!

Security specialists

Everyone in the store has to be involved in keeping things safe. But for some, it is the whole focus of their work. Security guards protect stock, check security systems, and also monitor people's safety. Shops and shopping centres rely on well-planned security systems and well-trained personnel to protect staff, customers, property, and **merchandise**. Security guards and store detectives are often employed by specialist companies who hire their services out to shopping centres and shops. Some stores prefer to recruit their own security guards.

Personal profile

◎ Good relationship with the public – after all they are all potential customers!
◎ Honest and discreet – knowing when to keep quiet about something or someone.
◎ Fit and able to be on your feet all day.
◎ An eye for detail and a good memory. A security guard or store detective must get to know quickly when something or someone is out of place.
◎ Highly disciplined, controlled, and calm – there is no room for "have-a-go heroes"!
◎ Knowledge of **surveillance** and arrest regulations.

What's in the job?

A security guard's duties depend on the premises. In a shopping centre, security staff patrol a "beat" – a set area – sorting out issues where necessary. Individual shop security guards patrol the shop and its exterior, focusing on particular hotspots and particular "clients". Security guards work with police to focus on known offenders, and identify problem areas and new offenders. A security manager in a shopping centre controls patrols and watches the whole area using a central CCTV camera network in the security office. A security guard can earn £7.00 per hour or more. Control room operators start on about £12,000 per year, and security managers for shopping centres can earn over £20,000.

Routes to recruitment

Some security guards are ex-armed service people and police. Others can enter the industry, but in most cases you have to be over 21. You will need evidence of a good all-round education if you want to be part of security. However, be prepared to do a course, because industry requirements now demand this.

You will need to study for one of several licences from the Security Industry Authority (SIA), depending on which area you are interested in. Store guards must have a licence, and the SIA offers modules in Retail. The course normally takes 4 days to complete. You can also study for an NVQ/SVQ Level 2 in Providing Security Services, which is specifically for work in retail.

Get ahead!

Want to become a store detective? If you are under 24, you could get an **apprenticeship**. Or with distance learning (an Internet or correspondence course), you could gain a Security Industry Training Organization (SITO) qualification to operate as a professional store detective. You can follow this up with a highly respected and practical Store Detectives' City and Guilds Certificate which can be gained either in-house or at a SITO centre. These days, most store detectives need an extra CCTV licence before they can use CCTV equipment. The International Professional Security Association runs a number of short training courses.

Chapter 5

The product

Do you ever wonder how some shops always seem to get it right? How they are always in fashion, have lots of choice, and sell at just the right **price point**? It is the role of the buyer that is key to making this happen.

Buyer

Buyers have to know about the products they are to buy and how much profit they are expected to make. Then they have to find the best quality products at the best price. Buyers also have to know where the products would sell well in the store, or in which particular part of the country. Do you have what it takes to fill this dynamic position?

Personal profile

◎ Analytical and shrewd – always one step ahead of fashions and trends.
◎ Confident, competitive, and a risk-taker.
◎ A good understanding of individuals and trends.
◎ Very good with figures – there is lots of sales data to look at.
◎ A good team player – you will be attending frequent planning meetings.
◎ Great organizational skills.
◎ Excellent presentation skills – both written and spoken, as you need to be very, very persuasive!

right: *Buyers can travel right to the place where the product grows in their quest to find the best products at the best prices.*

The aim of the game

In large supermarket chains and stores, a buyer will work within a product category. This could be something like fresh fruit and vegetables. The buyer starts the working week by reviewing category plans, sales figures, and financial targets. This means working with financial managers and sometimes with merchandisers, too. It is important to know exactly what everyone is trying to achieve. Then the buyer can make purchasing plans with confidence.

Knowing your product and customer

Plans include product placement. This means distributing products to particular stores in particular places. For example, some foods sell better in cities than in towns and in some parts of the country than in others. The buyer also has to make sure the timing is right when sourcing and buying goods. If the company misses a promotion, a trend or a season, then a lot of money is lost. A buyer really has to know the products well and work hard at finding a good-quality product at the right price. For some buyers, this can take them all over the world.

Buyers have to be on the ball. They have to respond quickly to sudden changes in the market and work hard at sourcing a new product if necessary. They must also be aware of public opinion and trends. **Kitemarking** and the moves toward **ethical sourcing** are good examples of this. Salary for junior buyers starts at about £16–18,000 per year, but the sky's the limit for senior buyers! The very best managers of buying departments can earn well over £50,000.

COMPETITIVE STREAK

In a supermarket or large chainstore, the buyer makes sure that their department makes the kind of profit expected. But a really ambitious buyer tries to take even more money than this, so their department gets given more floor space for its category. In other words, there can be a lot of internal competitiveness among buyers working for different departments in the same company. This motivates staff and drives sales and profit for the whole business. A successful buyer might get to manage a group of buying categories.

Some schools have asked buyers at local stores to be involved in Year 10 and 11 Design and Technology coursework projects. Perhaps yours could, too. For example, working in small teams, students could design and create a range of fashion wear for a particular season and age group. Using media studies skills, English, and ICT you pull together all your creative thinking, designs, and advertising tactics. Then you can plan a fashion show, inviting buyers to select the best range for the specification. This work can be properly **accredited** and put towards your exam success.

Routes to recruitment

Many trainee buyers have business degrees or BTEC qualifications with relevant retail modules. Some have degrees in Mathematics and Statistics. However, there are lots of people with these qualifications. So if you opt for the graduate route, make sure that you take advantage of as much work-based training as possible. Take that year's work experience placement if it is offered! Get a part-time job in retail, too. Many graduates without relevant work experience are being turned away.

left: *Buyers may need to travel all over the world to source a good-quality product.*

Getting the goods

If you react quickly to trends, are passionate about a product and how it is made, you could well become a merchandiser. This pacey, exciting job involves spotting trends, then creating the exact product or range that matches it. Part of the challenge is keeping within the retailer's brand image, the buyer's plan – and the budget!

Merchandiser

The merchandiser leads the design requirements of each product. So, for a garment, that means everything from its cut and colour to its fabric. The merchandiser follows the product's design and manufacture process and monitors its success on the shop floor. Product placement is essential for its success, so the merchandiser will help review where it goes in the store and in which store the product will succeed most. Sometimes the product's position in the store will change with the seasons. At other times, it will change with a sudden shift in trends. The product's price also needs to be reviewed constantly in line with competition and the product's popularity.

A junior merchandiser can start at between £16–18,000 per year. Senior merchandisers for large stores can earn £50,000 or more.

below: *Merchandisers have to get the quality and quantity of materials right, or a lot of money and energy may be wasted.*

Personal profile

◎ A passion for fashion – in whatever sphere that may be – from clothes to cosmetics to cushions. There is a fashion for every product and every product is associated with a design, even if it is just the packaging or the label.

◎ Determination to find the right materials for the right product, to achieve the right image for the brand.

◎ Excellent teamworking and presentation skills. You will have to work with buyers and designers, among others.

◎ A good instinct for trends and changes in trends, backed by lots of research.

◎ Awareness of the "Four Ps": product, price, promotion, and place.

Routes to recruitment

Most recruits are graduates. There are some very focused degree courses that you can take. They are sometimes geared to specific products. So, for instance, if you want to get into fashion merchandising, you could take a degree in Clothing Management and Technology. Many Design degrees either offer a Business module, or allow you to take Business for Design as the main course. But you also need good numeracy skills, as merchandisers deal with quantities and prices as well as quality, design, and materials. If a top merchandiser in a large organization gets the figures wrong, the company could lose a huge amount of money.

Alternative routes

There are some opportunities for moving sideways in a company to become a merchandiser. Alternatively you could work your way up after gaining other qualifications such as a BTEC National Award in Retail or Marketing. But these opportunities are shrinking. If you do want to follow this route, shop-floor experience is always valued, especially if it is with the product you wish to merchandise. Large organizations have whole merchandising departments with assistants, so there are sometimes openings there. As an assistant, you will need good word processing skills and OCR qualifications in specific software such as MS Word, Excel or Powerpoint.

Get ahead!

Try to include a merchandising project as part of your Year 10 and 11 coursework in Design and Technology. Some schools and colleges organize projects with merchandisers from local stores. As a team, students design and manufacture products within a budget and for a particular market. Using their ICT skills they present their merchandising plan and design to real merchandisers.

left: *Team discussion is an important part of a merchandiser's job – but decisions have to be made within a very limited time frame.*

Displaying the product

So, you have a flair for design and enjoy working on large-scale projects. Perhaps you like setting up displays in your school library? Or helping out with the scenery at your local amateur dramatic society? Are you a great team player and never get flustered? If so, you could be just right for the position of visual merchandiser.

above: *The end result of window dressing can look really artistic. But the display is cleverly planned to attract customers to certain products.*

Visual merchandiser

Visual merchandisers plan and design window and in-store displays and promotions. They also have to plan how products are arranged on the shelf. This means knowing the product, its size and quantity. Visual merchandisers also have to get to grips with all the fittings needed to display the product, and the point-of-sale that advertises it.

Personal profile
- ◎ Excellent **visual awareness** and a flair for design.
- ◎ Great teamworking skills.
- ◎ Numeracy and **spatial awareness** – designs and product placements have to fit specific spaces, fixtures, and fittings.
- ◎ A keen interest in advertising, especially brand image.

above: *Working out exactly how much product will go on a particular shelf can be really mind-bending. It is far easier to do it in a "dummy" store like this.*

Practise makes perfect!

Visual merchandisers in large chainstores practise their designs in a dummy store, which looks just like a real one. Here, they can see the impact of their designs – and can tweak them if needed. And there are no customers to stop their work! The visual merchandiser then uses a computer to create finished shelf plans, called **planograms**. These are clear designs that help replenishers and sales advisors to replenish shelves and set up promotions quickly and easily. The end result should always look full of product, with the promotion clearly highlighted.

right: *This planogram is promoting a "three-for-the-price-of-two" children's book offer. It includes activity and picture books for young children and fiction for teenagers, so different types of shelving have to be used.*

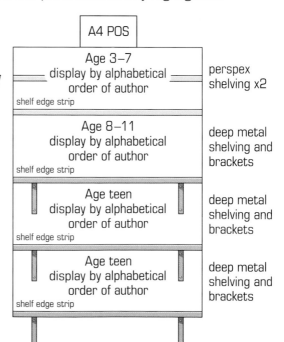

Brand awareness

Visual merchandisers need to be fully focused on their company's brand image and positioning within the retail world. They also have to be aware that companies often pay for the space and placement of a particular promotion

within a store. So it is crucial that the visual merchandiser understands the importance of agreements made between their store and the companies involved

Salary

A junior visual merchandiser starts at about £14,000 a year, while senior managers can earn £40,000 or more. There are often perks – such as a company car – for senior visual merchandisers. The job often involves a lot of travelling.

Routes to recruitment

GCSE Design and Technology (Graphics) can kickstart your move to become a visual merchandiser. There are BTEC retail modules in Visual Merchandising. These are very useful if you manage to get an apprenticeship. You will need good grades in Art, Design Technology, and Maths to get on a design course with a retail or merchandising module. Some companies recruit junior visual merchandisers from their stores, picking out staff who show a real flair for store presentation.

Chapter 6

From warehouse to store

Do you have what it takes to move the right stock in the right quantities at the right time from the warehouse to the store? This is a very difficult thing to achieve. The qualities of distribution managers and assistants are a key part of a company's success. Are you currently employed as a part-time replenisher? Does it give you a buzz when you have got everything in place and the store looks full and neat? If the answer is "Yes!", then maybe a job in distribution and logistics is for you.

Jobs in distribution

For large stores and chains, the warehouse operates on a sophisticated computerized system. **Product lines**, quantities, and destinations are all controlled from head office and managed on the ground by highly qualified staff. Distribution managers also assess the amount of storage space required, transport, and schedules. With perishable (easily spoiled or destroyed) items such as foodstuffs, storage conditions are monitored and transport has to be in refrigerated vans. For online shopping, products are usually stored in the company's warehouse, where they are packaged and despatched individually to customers. A distribution assistant could start at £12,000 a year. But a manager for a large chain could earn £50,000 a year or more.

Personal profile

◎ Teamwork and communication skills are essential. A distribution manager and assistants provide links between head office, suppliers, and stores, and also with drivers, who could be on the road anywhere in the country, or abroad.
◎ Distribution management requires excellent computer, technical, and logistical skills.

Routes to recruitment

You could start as a transport clerk, and for this you will need solid skills in Maths and English – good GCSEs in these would help. ICT skills will be essential, too. If you are under 24, try to get on an apprenticeship scheme. From this you could work your way up through a supervisor's role to higher management. While you are gaining experience you could study for NVQs/SVQs in Distribution, Warehousing and Storage Operations at Levels 2 and 3.

The Chartered Institute of Logistics and Transport (CILT) UK holds certificate, diploma, and higher diploma courses in Logistics and Transport. Or if you want to enter as a graduate trainee, a degree with modules in Transport, Logistics and Warehousing, or Supply Chain Management is highly desirable for acceptance on a graduate training scheme. Computer, Mathematics, and Geography qualifications are also possible ways in.

Moving up the ladder

A supply chain manager for a large retail organization might want to study for an MSc in Transport Planning and Management, or Supply Chain Management, or Logistics and Transport. The CILT offers continuing professional development (CPD) schemes for their members.

Get ahead!

If you are still at school and are interested in warehousing, try asking local warehouse managers which courses would be most relevant to a job in their particular organization. There are many courses and modules to choose from – from Distribution Control, Logistics, Operations, and Services to Exporting and Importing.

above: *Many retail businesses have more than one warehouse. Their activities are coordinated by well-qualified distribution managers.*

Warehouse worker

Are you really methodical, a good team player, and very fit? Then you could begin warehouse work as a loader and stacker. Most training is on-the-job. You will learn storage methods and how to use and put together the fittings and fixtures needed for particular products. You will also learn health and safety regulations, how to lift goods and use lifting equipment. If you are over 18 you can be trained to use a lift truck. It is also important to learn fire regulations and the requirements of fire safety inspectors for your premises. Completing paperwork and checking off products is an important part of keeping a tight rein on supplies. You could also be trained to use specific computer software and **intranet** communications. Warehouse workers can earn anything from the minimum wage to £7.00 per hour or more.

Get ahead!

You could work towards a supervisory position through NVQs/SVQs Levels 2 and 3 in Distribution, Warehousing and Storage Operations, or in Storage and Warehousing. Day-release courses can help you gain a Chartered Institute of Logistics and Transport Level 2 Introductory Certificate in Logistics and Transport. It has a really useful optional Warehousing module. Warehouse workers with good GCSE grades in Maths and IT will normally be encouraged to take team leader positions. A BTEC National Award in Retail can help you along this trail. Supervisors might well need a relevant Level 3 Higher Certificate in Logistics and Transport. A clean driving licence is often helpful.

below: *Boxes all tend to look the same. Warehouse workers get to know different suppliers' box labels quickly. It speeds up movement of deliveries.*

Routes to recruitment

Good basic English, Maths, and IT skills are desirable – warehouse work is increasingly high-tech. Storage is often colour-coded, so a colour vision test might be given at interview. Under 24s can take advantage of apprenticeship schemes.

Driver

Are you very active, flexible, disciplined, punctual, good-humoured, and love to travel? Yes? Then working as a delivery driver might be just for you. Drivers are crucial to retail. They make sure that the right product arrives in the right place at the right time. Delays or mistakes can often mean that a shop misses out on a crucial promotion. This can mean huge losses to a business.

Personal profile

◎ Good teamworking and flexibility.
◎ Sound geographical knowledge and route planning.
◎ Knowledge of **hauliers**' regulations, for example there are **statutory** stoppage times for heavy goods vehicle (HGV) drivers, meaning they must take regular breaks from driving.
◎ Knowledge of health and safety regulations.
◎ Excellent timekeeping and reliability.
◎ A cool head. Alternative routes and instructions – and traffic jams – are common challenges.

Delivery details

Drivers have to make sure that their deliveries are packed in the correct sequence and properly marked for their destination. Warehouse workers often load the delivery trucks, but if the sequence is wrong, the driver wastes time finding the correct delivery. Goods are often packed in cages or on to **pallets**, ready to be wheeled into a store's stockroom. The number of pallets and cages or boxes and bags is usually marked on the delivery note and the driver's written schedule. So a driver must be happy dealing with paperwork.

On the road

Once everything is ready, the driver sets off. Many drivers have to travel long distances, from central distribution to the individual stores in towns and cities across the country. Some also have to travel abroad. Drivers are expected to complete a given circuit of stores within a certain time. They have to arrive in good time so that crates, cages, and pallets can be offloaded and counted. A driver's earnings start at about £6.50 per hour. Grade 1 HGV drivers can earn from £18,000 per year. A transport manager's salary can be £35,000.

Routes to recruitment

You might have to wait to become a driver, as most companies only take on over-21s. Some only take drivers aged 25 and over. Drivers must have clean HGV licences and good personal references.

below: *Drivers have to unload and check off stock quickly. They have timesheets that monitor how long they take between each drop.*

Get ahead!

See if you would like the challenge of navigating long distances! You could work out the best route to get to your next holiday destination – and find the quickest routes to avoid congestion in your town at peak periods.

Chapter 7

Recruitment and training

One of the main tasks of human resources (HR) personnel is to help find the right person for the right job. They also help shape and achieve a company's aims and working practices through recruitment plans and job outlines. They develop jobs by reworking personal specifications, expectations, and grading schemes. HR moves industry standards forward through training sessions and manuals and by constantly updating job descriptions. Training can include group role-playing sessions and finding solutions to specific problems within a retail environment.

Working in HR

HR personnel have to know the business and what motivates people to really do their best. A human resources assistant's starting salary is usually about £15,000 per year. An area manager for HR earns on average £35,000. A first-class HR manager or trainer can earn a top salary – £50,000 per year and more.

below: *Many HR departments will be involved with organizing the fun side of work, such as the annual staff party.*

Personal profile

- Passionate about people, especially in their role as workers.
- Passionate about retail and about training for excellence.
- Excellent communication and motivation skills.
- Excellent, clear writing skills for job specifications and training programmes.
- Excellent teamwork skills to engage all sides of the business in recruiting and **upskilling**.
- Shop-floor experience. This helps you to understand time limits on in-store training for management and staff.

Routes to recruitment

A degree is almost essential these days. There are specialist degree courses in Human Resources. Psychology is also considered a very good choice. You will need a good understanding of the qualities that different people need for different jobs.

A different angle

There are different strands to HR work, so it can appeal to people with very different skills. If you are good with facts and figures, filing, and using computer software packages, then record-keeping and issuing contracts might be for you. These are often linked closely to payroll (salaries) work. For this type of job, good ICT and maths skills are essential. You can provide evidence of this through OCR qualifications and through GCSEs in ICT and Maths. Your salary could start at around £10,000 to £12,000 per year.

Get ahead!

You will need to demonstrate excellent verbal communication and motivational abilities, and team leadership. Helping out during the holiday at a children's playgroup, or something similar, could help increase these skills. Good, clear, organized writing is important. You could practise for this by making sure that your non-fiction assignments, such as History or Geography, are well structured, methodical, and clear. Understanding the importance of customer service is probably the most important thing of all. Try to get a weekend job in retail. It really will help.

Retail trainer

Do you make sure that you take an interest in everything that you tackle, from organizing a night out to tidying your room and doing homework?! Are you the kind of person who can really get other people involved with a project or an event? If so, you could be perfect as a retail trainer. But what do retail trainers do?

above: *A training session can sometimes open up a new side to a person. It can change things about their life as well as their job prospects.*

Elaine Oliver, Retail Training and Development Manager, New Look

New Look is one of the world's most popular fashion retailers. The company has over 700 stores worldwide, with 169 million customers in the UK and 11,000 workers! It is Elaine's job to enthuse all those employees. How on earth does she manage to do it? Well, she succeeds because she loves motivating people. And she loves fashion retail, too. Elaine's passion for people and what they wear makes her a constant people-watcher – from the minute she sets off to work, through her lunch break and on her way home again! She also keeps her eye on national and global issues. So Elaine brings a lot of up-to-date knowledge and freshness to her work. This includes brand workshops, focus groups, and induction courses that she organizes and runs. She also brings this knowledge to her meetings with company directors, training managers, and coordinators, and to the training programmes that she writes.

Elaine sees training as a way of helping the company to grow and develop from within, using the skills and talents of the employees. Her own background includes a degree in Psychology and a teacher training certificate. She has worked in other retail environments, training replenishers in a supermarket, bravely facing customers on a Christmas hamper complaint line, and then as a regional training manager. Now, she is at the top of the training tree. But she is as enthusiastic as ever!

below: *Some companies offer their staff team-building courses like this one. These courses help staff to get on and work well together.*

Chapter 8

Going it alone

Got a great idea for a shop? Want to set up your own retail business? Excellent! But going it alone is a lot of hard work. You will need to plan well ahead, but be prepared to think on your feet as well. Communication skills are vital, as you will probably have to deal with bankers, suppliers, the Inland Revenue (Government's tax office), builders, and lots more besides. But most of all you will need a determined, positive attitude.

What about the salary? For the first year or two, most of the profits are ploughed back into the business. Many take on other jobs to help finance their dream. But if their idea works, then the sky is the limit!

Here are two real examples of people who have successfully pursued their ideas.

Shop owner

Mel Pye not only wanted to set up a retail business, she also wanted to provide a service – to customers and to her home town. So Mel made plans to open up a specialist children's shoe shop, Neet Feet, in an area of Dover that is being developed. She knew there was a gap in the market for that type of shop, and was determined to offer excellent customer service to children.

Determination

At first, Mel had problems getting premises. There were plenty of empty shops but the agents wouldn't take her seriously, even though she had a solid business plan. But Mel never gave up. She approached a shop owner direct, and managed to buy the lease.

Growing the business

Mel went to trade fairs to buy her stock. She managed to get most of it without having to pay for it all up front. This helped her to keep enough money to last for the first 6 months of trading.

After paying bills and staffing costs, Mel ploughs back her profits into the business. Once Mel is well in profit, she hopes to open up another Neet Feet. Her shop looks great and is an asset to the town – and to children's feet. Mel admits she is a real perfectionist, and it shows!

Learning as you go

Mel says that if she did it over again, she would definitely leave more time for refurbishing the premises. The night before opening day she was up until 4 a.m. getting everything ready! Mel also now road-tests all the shoes – trying them out on children's feet before buying them in. When she first opened, some styles looked great but needed to fit better.

Get ahead!

Mel recommends that you take advantage of the many business and accounting courses on offer. A lot of these are free – and some only take a few hours to complete. For example, her local Inland Revenue office holds courses for filling in **VAT** and **PAYE** forms. Mel also took a 6-month part-time course to help her prepare her business plan, among other useful skills. It was run by the New Entrepreneur Scheme (NES). Mel won the NES Retail Business of the Year Award in 2005.

above: *Setting up your own shop can be a lot of hard work, but will make you feel extremely proud.*

Online retailer

UK Christmas online sales through the Internet can currently take nearly £5 billion, and as many as 40 per cent of shoppers try to buy all their gifts in this way. One young **entrepreneur** had an idea to sell items associated with the Buddhist faith, such as prayer beads, online. This is how he created his own Internet shop.

Steps to success

First, Ben researched the kinds of products he wanted to sell, and how they were currently sold online. Could he improve on existing websites? He then studied **wholesalers**' websites and catalogues to find supplies of the right products at the right price. A careful selection was made, with prices to suit most pockets. He then created his own website using **HyperText Mark-up Language** (HTML) and photographs of his product that he took himself, using a digital camera. Doing this work himself saved Ben a lot of money, which he has used to buy stock.

Getting technical

Ben needed to find a bank that specializes in online sales – one that makes sure the site is secure before any purchases are made. He paid an Internet server to place the website on the Internet. Ben then integrated the banking facility and shopping basket onto his website and tested the whole buying process. After this was working he made sure that customers could find the website through other related websites and search engines.

Strong background

Ben read free websites on the Internet to learn how to use HTML and set up a website. Having a GCSE in Maths meant he could get to grips with the figures. He also had a lot of sales and customer service experience through jobs in retail and in the service and entertainment sectors. This definitely shows in his well-planned, user-friendly website. One of the best things about his site is his knowledge of the products and the background information behind them.

Get ahead!

Getting your head around figures is really important if you want to set up on your own. Business studies are a good option at A-level (England and Wales) and Highers (Scotland). Computer literacy is a huge benefit, too. Understanding computer languages such as HTML is essential if you want to create a website yourself – you will save a lot of money.

below: *A website can be a great way to advertise and sell your products.*

Chapter 9

Onwards and upwards

What can retail lead to? In-store experience is recognized by other fields as excellent for the development of interpersonal skills. Customer service and aftercare skills are especially valuable. Good interpersonal skills open up avenues in other careers such as reception work, library assistant work, tourist and information office work, and call-centre aftercare. In fact, anything that involves personal interaction with clients, whether in the **public sector** or **private sector**.

left: *Skills learned in retail can really help you get on in jobs where contact with the public is the biggest part of your working day.*

Get ahead!

Retail experience can lead to careers in other areas such as personal assistant (PA) work, human resources (HR), and local government. OCR qualifications in word processing packages such as Microsoft Word and Excel can help you get this type of job. At management level, retail experience is highly valued in the public sector.

Work experience schemes

Are you taking advantage of your school's work experience scheme? Most schools organize work experience placements for students in Year 10 or 11. Some students find their own placements, or are helped by their parents. You won't always be given the placement of your choice. But you will get a really good idea of a working environment. And you will get to use a lot of your schoolwork and skills in the "real world", too.

left: *All your experiences in life can prepare you for working in retail. They will help you to understand people, which is what retail is all about.*

Stepping into work

Your school will prepare you for your work experience placement. You will cover issues of health and safety, the route to work, what to wear, and what to expect. Preparation will include showing you how to record your experiences, new skills gained, and positive and negative points. A diary, charts, and graphs of your progress are useful additions to your workplace portfolio.

Work experience placements vary hugely. The best are those where you get a taster of different aspects of a job, or different departments within a store. You will be supervised by a worker experienced in each task or within each department. You shouldn't be expected to do anything you haven't been shown how to do properly. Nor are you there to slog for 8 hours in place of someone who is off sick! A teacher from your school will come and visit you in your workplace to check your progress. Most placements are really positive experiences.

Getting noticed

You are really keen to get into retail. You did your Year 10 work experience placement in a local newsagents and really enjoyed it. There is a weekend sales assistant vacancy in the accessories department at a large store. So you go in and ask for an application form. You turn up smiling, and you are very polite.

Filling in the form

Now it's time to show that you are just right for the job. Time to fill in that application form! If you can't get one directly from the store, most chains, department stores and supermarkets can send one from Head Office. Some forms can be filled in online, too.

Companies want to find out very specific things about you. So before you launch into your application, read the form very carefully. Always do as it asks! For instance, if you are meant to write within a box and in capital letters, then it is wise to do so. Firstly, it's easier to read. Secondly, it shows that you can follow instructions. This is very important in the retail world!

The forms are designed firstly to find out basic information – your date of birth, qualifications, and so on. Then, there are usually sections that enable you to really show that you are the right person for the job that's been advertised. Sometimes you are given the chance to say more about yourself by adding an extra page of writing. Try to keep this focused on how your experiences meet the needs of the job and the retail trade.

For instance, you might be applying for a job as a replenisher in a fruit and vegetable department in a large supermarket. Perhaps you have travelled extensively – maybe to southern Europe and the Caribbean. You could mention briefly on the form that you can name and recognize most fruits and vegetables from these regions - and have tasted many of them, too. This is important to the job, as a lot of produce is imported from these areas.

Perhaps you have worked as a volunteer in the school library, stacking books on shelves. This is also relevant. You know how to put out stock properly and in a particular order.

Remember that companies are looking for enthusiasm and an interest in retail. If you can mention that you would be really focused on customer service and product knowledge, this can go a long way. If you can give evidence of being a good team player and a reliable worker, this will also give you a big tick.

Covering letters and CVs

You might want to apply to a shop or store even if there are no jobs advertised. For instance, perhaps you want to get a summer vacation job and know that it is best to apply well ahead. Or you might be leaving school in the summer and want to get a foothold on the retail ladder. For this, you will need to send a CV and covering letter to your chosen stores. Most chains, department stores, and supermarkets have their own websites that will tell you how to apply to their company. So it's best to consult these before you start your CV and covering letter. But for other shops, you can study what each sells, the service it gives, the attitudes of the staff, how the shop presents its stock, and so on. Then you can write your covering letter and CV in a way that shows how you fit into that shop's profile and needs. There is a sample covering letter and a CV on pages 49 and 50. You can tweak them according to the kind of business you are applying to.

A sample covering letter

A covering letter isn't meant to replace a CV, but it does give you the chance to introduce yourself and outline your qualities. It also enables you to show how you would fit in to a particular store and working environment. Through the letter you can demonstrate that you understand the nature of the business you are applying to. On the opposite page you can see a suitable letter layout, contents and length.

Megan Lowe
56 Cheriton
Rugby
Warwickshire WB1 5RH
Tel: 02430 363151

30 March 2006

Mr M Khan
Music Matters
5-7 High Street
Rugby
Warwickshire
WB1A 4WX

Dear Mr Khan

Sales Advisor's position

I am hoping to start a career in music retail when I leave school this summer. I enclose my CV with this letter and hope that you will be able to consider me for any upcoming Sales Advisor vacancies. I have experience of working in a retail environment and I am keen to offer good customer service as well as undertake tasks. I am punctual and have a good attendance record.

I am often a customer at Music Matters and find that it has a really relaxed atmosphere with a friendly and helpful staff. Your store offers an excellent selection of music. As you can see from my CV, I have a keen interest in many types of music, particularly Garage and Hip Hop. I also play the classical guitar. My passion for music means that I am really keen to acquire good product knowledge and satisfy the customer by finding the right music for their needs.

I am a flexible, cheerful team worker and relish new challenges. I am happy to work to any shift pattern, including weekends.

Yours sincerely

MLowe

Megan Lowe

Megan Lowe

Date of birth	14 September 1990
Address	56 Cheriton Rugby Warwickshire WB1 5RH
Telephone	02430 363151
Email	meganlowe@email.net
School	Ringwood School and Technology College Wright's Lane Rugby Warwickshire WB2 6RA

EDUCATION

GCSEs	Estimated Grade
English Language	B
English Literature	B
French	D
Humanities	B
Mathematics	C
Music	A
Science (Double Award)	B

Computer Qualification   OCR First Certificate in Computing, 2006

Music Qualification   Classic Guitar ABSM Certificate Grade 7, 2005

Other Qualifications
First Aid Certificate, 2006
Life Saving Certificate, 2006

EMPLOYMENT/WORK EXPERIENCE

- Saturday job at a local newsagent's, from September 2005:
  My job includes customer service, operating the till, and tasks. The tasks include newspaper recalls and replenishment, replenishment of other stock such as sweets and groceries, and pricing goods. I take newspaper orders and sort out papers for the paper round. I tidy, sweep the floor, and dust the shelves.

- Two weeks' work experience placement in a kitchen shop in a large department store in June 2004:
  My experience included customer service, helping customers to find the right product. I also wrapped goods at the till point. I helped to replenish the stock, price goods, clean shelves, and put up fittings.

HOBBIES AND INTERESTS

I help out in a music workshop for children every Thursday evening. We are putting on a concert this summer. I also belong to a rambler's club. Last year we walked in the French Pyrenees. At home I enjoy reading and playing music with my friends.

REFERENCES

Work reference:	Personal reference:
Mrs Martha Barnes	Mr L Carey (Year 11 Tutor)
Martha's Mags	Ringwood School and Technology College
121 Longden Road	Wright's Lane
Rugby	Rugby
Warwickshire WB1A 6BS	Warwickshire WB2 6RA
Tel: 02430 378959	Tel: 02430 552661

Interviews

Well done, you've got an interview! Now for the preparation. What will you wear? Think about the kinds of clothes you feel confident in (not just comfortable in!) If you are going for a job in a store, take a good look at what the management is wearing before your interview. Some are really "suited and booted". So a smart, dark jacket would be appropriate, with a decent pair of trousers or skirt and neat, clean shoes. In a more informal store, an open-neck shirt with a smart jacket but no tie would probably work well. Just make it look as if you have really thought about it. Your hair needs to be clean and tidy. Makeup should be applied with care – and not too obvious.

What shall I say?

Prepare questions as well as answers. Take a good look at the store to give you clues about the product and work involved. Good questions to start with are about the products you will be dealing with. How varied will your work be? Will there be opportunities to upskill? How do you

progress? Is progression through the company's grading schemes or through NVQs/SVQs? Never make money the first issue on your agenda. It just makes you look desperate and disinterested in the work itself. Towards the end of the interview you could ask, "Please could you clarify the pay scale and grade of this position for me?"

left: *Make sure you arrive about ten minutes before your interview time, so you have a chance to settle your nerves and don't look flustered.*

Most large retailers have their own websites with careers advice and job advertisements. Just tap in their company name on your search engine, and you should get access to them. Or you can go to your local store and find out what the website is.

Retail organizations and websites
Education and training

You can find out about education and training for retail from the following websites. Qualifications and schemes of work are always changing, so it is best to keep checking them out yourself.

◎ Department For Education and Science
(www.dfes.gov.uk)
◎ EDEXCEL
www.edexcel.org.uk
◎ learndirect
(www.learndirect-advice.co.uk)
◎ National Council for Work Experience
(www.work-experience.org)
◎ Qualifications and Curriculum Authority (QCA)
(www.qca.org.uk)
◎ Skillsmart Retail
(www.skillsmartretail.com)
– This is the Sector Skills Council for Retail. It works with retailers to attract enthusiastic and talented people into the industry.
◎ TTC Training
(www.ttctraining.co.uk/retail.htm)
◎ UK National Reference Point for Vocational Qualifications
(www.uknrp.org.uk)

Transport, distribution and logistics
◎ Association of Industrial Truck Trainers
(www.aitt.co.uk)
◎ The Chartered Institute of Logistics and Transport
(www.ciltuk.org.uk)

Retail and rights

You should always be treated with dignity at work – and you should also treat others with dignity. Your development needs should also be met. Trades unions (organizations set up to protect workers' rights and working conditions) and voluntary support organizations in retail can always advise you on these and other issues. They have good information on training, too.

◎ Union of Shop, Distributive and Allied Workers (USDAW)
(www.usdaw.org.uk)
– This is the largest retail trade union, with over 340,000 members.
◎ Retail Book Association
(www2.the-rba.org)
– The RBA represents thousands of bookshop workers.
◎ Retail Trust
(www.retailtrust.org.uk)
– Retail Trust is the national charity for the retail industry.
It provides advice and support for those in retail, or those thinking about retail as a career.

Books and magazines

◎ Clark, Val. *How To Start and Run Your Own Shop*
(How To Books, 2005)
◎ Paulins, V. Ann., and Julie L. Hillery. *Professional Development for Retailing and Apparel Merchandising* (Fairchild Books, 2006)
◎ Seliet, Hala. *BTEC Introduction to Business, Retail and Administration* (Heinemann, 2005)
◎ Tucker, Johnny. *Retail Desire: Design Display and the Art of the Visual Merchandiser* (Rotovision, 2004)
◎ Retail Week magazine (www.retail-week.com)
– This is really useful for those who want an in-depth look at what is going on in UK retailing. It is quite a hard read, but shows who the "movers and shakers" are and what the most pressing issues are at the moment.

accredited   given a qualification for work you have done, often as part of a course

aftercare   advice for the customer on the returns policy, the product itself, or other products that might go with it

apprenticeship   training scheme that allows you to work for money, learn, and become qualified at the same time

brand   trademark and tradename with a strong image

branding   creating a strong image for a tradename through things like design, logos, and slogans

BTEC   Business and Technician Education Council. The qualifications it awards include the Higher National Certificate (HNC) and Higher National Diploma (HND).

budget   set amount of money used to achieve something

concessions   shops that rent space within a large department store. The shops usually belong to a chain.

covering letter   letter that introduces you to an employer, accompanying your CV

curriculum vitae   (CV) one or two sheets of paper with information about you, your skills, and your achievements

day-release   course or work experience placement that takes you out of your normal work or school routine for a day each week

entrepreneur   someone who invests in a business, either their own or someone else's

ethical sourcing   finding materials and products to sell that have been made by people working in decent conditions and for a fair wage

hauliers   companies that have fleets of lorries that transport goods

HyperText Mark-up Language (HTML) computer language used to create documents for the Internet

interpersonal skills   ability to relate well to other people

intranet   closed Internet system that links computers within an organization

logistics   working out detailed plans to get goods to the right place at the right time

kitemarking   marking goods with a kite shape to show that they conform to British Standards Institution regulations

merchandise   product for sale; also a verb meaning to sell a product

merchandiser   person employed to set up the creation and supply of a particular product

National Vocational Qualification   (NVQ) in England and Wales, a work-related, competence-based qualification that shows you have the knowledge and skills to do a job effectively. NVQs represent standards that are recognized by employers throughout the UK.

outlets shops that buy in goods from other retailers at a low price. You can get some good designer bargains in these!

Oxford, Cambridge and RSA (OCR) one of the UK's leading awarding bodies

pallets flat wooden slatted blocks on which delivery boxes are carried

PAYE Pay as You Earn – system of government taxation, where the tax is taken directly out of your pay

planograms plans of shelves showing placement of products

point-of-sale written information, such as price, offer, name of product, etc., set up where the product is displayed

price point price set for a particular product at a particular time – worked out to attract customers but still make profit

private sector organizations paid for privately (not by the Government)

product line particular product bought into a store, often as part of a range. Each line has its own line number recorded on the bar code, till, and store computer.

product placement putting a product in the most effective part of the store to make the most sales

promotion highlighting a particular product at a particular time, advertising its price and benefits

public sector organizations paid for by the Government

references written or verbal support for your job application from individuals who know you or have worked with you

Scottish Vocational Qualification (SVQ) in Scotland, a work-related, competence-based qualification that shows you have the knowledge and skills to do a job effectively. SVQs represent standards that are recognized by employers throughout the UK.

spatial awareness ability to see how space can best be used to present products and displays

statutory required by law

surveillance careful, planned watch kept on a person or place

upskill develop existing skills or gain new ones

VAT Value Added Tax – a tax on the amount by which the value of a product has increased at each stage of its production or distribution

visual awareness very good eye for presentation and detail

wholesaler company that sells products and materials in bulk

application forms
47–48
apprenticeships 22,
33, 35

brand awareness 31
business and
accounting courses
42
buyers 23–25

call-centre selling 13
career advancement
45
career choice 9
career planning
15–19
chain stores 5, 14, 24,
30, 48
communication skills
13, 32, 38, 41
computer literacy 44
control room operators
21
customer care 13,
14, 45
customer expectations
6
CVs and covering
letters 8, 48–50

day-release schemes 9
degree courses 27, 38
distribution assistants
32
distribution and
logistics 32–36
distribution managers
32
dress code 51
drivers 35–36

graduates 25, 27, 33

human resources (HR)
assistants 37

human resources (HR)
managers 37
human resources (HR)
personnel 37–38

ICT skills 14, 38
Internet 43–44
interviews 51

jobs in the retail
industry 5

lift truck drivers 34
loaders and stackers
34

management positions
15–19, 21, 32,
33, 36
merchandisers 26–28
merchandising
assistants 28
multi-tasking 12, 13
mystery shoppers 14

NVQs/SVQs 6–7

online retailers 43–44

pay 11, 14, 16, 21,
24, 26, 31, 32, 36,
37, 38, 51
personal qualities and
skills 10, 13, 15, 17,
20, 23, 27, 29, 32,
35, 38
planograms 30
product placement
24, 26

qualifications 6–7, 13

recruitment and
training positions
37–40

replenishers
10–11, 47
retail calendar 8
retail trainers 39–40

sales advisors 12–14
school subjects 14
security guards 20,
21, 22
security managers 21
security specialists
20–22
self-employment
41–43
shop owners 41–42
store detectives
20, 22
store managers
16–17
supermarkets 5, 14,
24, 48
supervisors 15–16
supply chain
managers 33

team-building courses
40
teamworking 13, 23,
27, 31, 32, 38
transferable skills 45
transport clerks 33
transport managers
36

visual merchandisers
29–31

Wal-mart 5
warehouse workers
34–35
warehousing 32–35
weekend and holiday
jobs 10, 12
work experience 9, 46

Titles in the *How to get ahead in* series include:

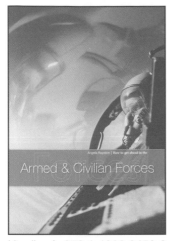

Hardback 978 1 4062 0450 6

Hardback 978 1 4062 0448 3

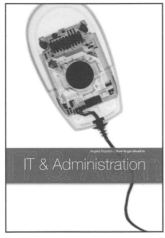

Hardback 978 1 4062 0449 0

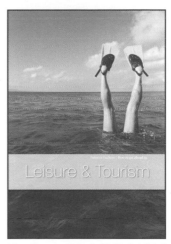

Hardback 978 1 4062 0447 6

Hardback 978 1 4062 0446 9

Other titles available:

Beauty	Hardback 978 1 4062 0442 1
Catering	Hardback 978 1 4062 0443 8
Construction	Hardback 978 1 4062 0440 7
Engineering and Design	Hardback 978 1 4062 0441 4
Healthcare	Hardback 978 1 4062 0444 5

Find out about the other titles in this series on our website at www.raintreepublishers.co.uk